C000165045

The Magical World of YOU!

The Magical World of **YOU!**

Your Guide to Self-Worth, Self-Love and Success.

Sarah Marie Park

Contents

Acknowledgments

I dedicate this book to anyone who is willing to embark on an amazing journey of self-discovery, self-love and self-belief. Despite your past struggles, your life will improve in miraculous ways when you commit to being your own biggest fan. This book is your encouragement to explore life outside of your comfort zone.

THANK YOU for choosing 'The Magical World of YOU!'

To anyone who has ever rejected or doubted me in the past –

THANK YOU! Thank you for allowing me to walk away and improve my life, as parting ways paved the way for my happiness and success.

I give special thanks and dedication to my Mum and Dad. I am forever grateful to you both, for giving us the best life, and for always believing in our dreams.

You have never doubted me and my (sometimes crazy) ideas and have always provided the ears and the voices that helped to guide me through life's projects.

THANK YOU.

I thank my husband for loving me unconditionally, and for supporting my hobbies, my career choices, and my dreams.

You have taught me to embrace myself as I am, and you have pushed me to become the best version of myself.

THANK YOU.

I thank my son. You are the inspiration for EVERYTHING that I do. You have made my life complete in ways that I cannot explain, and you have shown me the meaning of eternal love.

I cannot wait to see what greatness you achieve, as you continue to grow and become more amazing with each day. My mini-Einstein!

THANK YOU.

I thank myself, Sarah for putting in the work! For pushing through the 'off' days, for realising my own worth and for taking the necessary risks to pursue all of my own goals – all while staying true to myself.

THANK YOU.

I thank God for blessing me with my amazing life and the amazing opportunities that come with it. It is the faith and trust in you, that grants all of my wishes.

THANK YOU.

Enjoy the journey...

Introduction

So here we are... You and I uniting via this very book!

This is because something (or someone) has prompted you to read it. Rest assured that my book is in your life for a reason...

A beautiful, positive reason nonetheless, and if you are already familiar with self-development tools, you may be wondering how my book will differ to so many others out there.

Well...

I believe that the key to living a positive, fulfilled life, is to be consistently happy and to continually take new steps to becoming a better person (and therefore living a better life).

Hopefully my writing style will make certain things 'click' for you and help you to keep the manifesting momentum going.

I want to ensure that every reader takes something positive away from the upcoming chapters, as I have made it my mission as an Author (so this is non-negotiable I'm afraid!)

My aim *literally* is to help you achieve your goals and to assist in making all of your dreams come true!

Now then... although I am not claiming to be some world-renowned Guru, I can confidently state that my wisdom, education, past experiences, and passion for helping others to believe in themselves, stand me in good stead when getting this point across:

Your dream life really is in your own hands.

It TRULY IS!

By sharing my own life hacks and realisation of the Law of Attraction (LOA), I wish for you to see that any blockages in your life, any obstacles, traumas or bad experiences can indeed be dealt with and overcome.

You just need to be aware of your own mindset and control your own reactions to the events that surround you.

It's as simple as that, as long as you are willing to:

- Open and expand your mind,
- Accept that the tasks in this book do work,
- Try ALL of them out – with faith and excitement,
- Put in the effort when working towards your goals,
- Switch the narrative,
- Cut out negative, habitual behaviours - (the kind of behaviours that do no good for anyone!)

It is never too late to make positive life tweaks, and to choose the right path for a better future.

Remember that no one else on this planet is YOU and you can determine your own future.

You therefore have the power to make the chapters in your own real-life personal story, nothing less than sensational!

The homework sections are there to ensure that you are doing YOUR bit and putting my suggestions into practise.

There is no point reading about and thinking about positive changes, without actually putting the work in yourself.

I say this, because in this day and age, a lot of people sit all day long scrolling through social media, wishing they could have what others have!

More and more people are becoming aware of the concept of manifesting things and the term 'dream, believe, achieve', but I often find that people will read a book, shout from the rooftops that they're now on a positive growth journey and then what happens?

They sit down, do nothing and **wait** for a miracle to happen (without actively changing a thing!) The novelty (or trend) seems to wear off unfortunately.

Miracles do indeed happen, and yes, your biggest dreams can take months to appear (or years), but dreams and miracles are formed with the presence of ALL of the following:

- Self-love,

- Determination,

- Patience,

- Trial & Error,

- Gratitude,

- Teamwork,

- Happiness,

- Love,

- Belief.

As the great Albert Einstein said;

"Insanity is doing the same thing over and over again and expecting different results"

If you think outside the box, find the confidence to try new things, take the risks and dare be different to everyone else, you will introduce yourself to new possibilities.

Please don't ever be too afraid to:

- Question things,

- Try new things,

- Stand out from the crowd,

If you don't do these things, you risk hiding behind the 'shoulda, woulda, coulda' excuse if someone else goes ahead and creates or suggests what you decided not to!

Einstein was just a normal person (an amazing, influential hero nonetheless), but his ideas and actions were dubbed as crazy back in his day.

Did you know that despite formally requesting to be cremated, his wishes were ignored?!

This was simply because Scientists wanted to remove his brain and find out what was different or 'wrong' with it.

All because he was a genius!

His brain was cut up, examined and later used in a medical museum.

Turns out, he did not have some 'one of a kind' supersonic robot brain (like some wanted to believe).

His brain was in fact, nothing out of the ordinary.

He just brought amazing life to his imagination, his beliefs and his intentions – thus allowing the world to understand the complexities of the universe, gravity, space and time.

Miraculous!

My absolute key point that I need you to remember here, is that you must NEVER give up or undervalue your own talents.

Never be worried about what others may think. YOU are number one.

You can be the next person to make history - whatever your unique gift(s) may be.

You must embrace all the failures and rejections, and look for the silver lining in every challenging situation.

EVERYONE has setbacks along their journeys to success.

You must never lose faith, as the moment you stop believing (just because something hasn't landed on your doorstep that very week or month), you lose all momentum and your old, unfulfilled life will resume.

Masterpieces are not always created overnight and "Rome wasn't built in a day" but the bricks were constantly being laid.

Little steps are indeed ***steps*** - towards progress and fulfilment, so just keep building those foundations.

A joint effort between YOU and the universe is what will ensure that things (and people) in your life, align perfectly. In such a manner that paves the way for your dream life.

Sitting at home scrolling through someone else's life is not going to bring you the things you crave.

What you must do, is make a stand.

Get off your ass and start moving!

Whether it's moving around and physically exercising to improve your mood and to stimulate blood flow and productivity...

Or moving that pen across paper to outline a plan...

Just do something!

All small wins become larger wins when you move forward with intention and belief, so carry on with those baby steps each day.

When I was a child (born in the early 80's) my 2 older brothers and I would forever be outdoors in nature, living our best lives!

Crawling in the fields, making dens, playing with insects, climbing trees, swinging, sliding and playing ball games.

That was the life! And it taught us a lot. These days, I find it sad to see most kids glued to electronic devices in their free time, with limited time outdoors.

I am certainly not judging anyone here, as I know that such devices have great purpose at times (and in particular, when you just need to get something done for yourself!)

I totally get it - they keep kids occupied. What I am saying however, is that there should be a healthy balance. This way, kids (and adults alike) do not become so disconnected with the outdoor world that they miss out on physical, educational, cultural...

And most importantly, **FUN** activities (with real people!)

If you are amongst the many folk that *does* spend a lot of time scrolling through social sites, or if you simply feel bored or dissatisfied with your life/job/friends/home (or anything else), then it's time to make a change.

So although this book is classed as a self-help guide, look at it as more of a real account of life, love and happiness... From a normal, middle-aged Stokie bird!

Middle-aged? How the heck did that happen?!

Wow! It feels like I was in school only yesterday.

That's how quickly life can whiz by, so we must stop and appreciate it at any given opportunity.

Don't be so busy stressing about the insignificant things that you forget to live life to the fullest.

So you may be thinking 'what the heck does she know about life?', and let me just make it clear at this point...

I am not going to delve too deep into the LOA, or neuroscience (there are lots more specialised books for that) but let's just say that the LOA is the whole reason I am here as a self-published Author!

I dreamed, I believed and I achieved – in *SO* many areas of my life!

You can too.

Let's take a look at how our thoughts become reality.

Do you ever look at your life and think "Wow, I dreamt of being in this position when I was younger"?

I certainly do!

If you are shaking your head in disagreement and maintaining that your life is *not* amazing, or maybe you are doubting that manifestation works, then ask yourself the following questions:

1. Are you currently studying to better yourself?

If yes - YOU took action to make this happen! You decided on a pathway (whether it came via your career, or a hobby) and you are now working towards furthering your own knowledge and qualifications.

You are growing and evolving as a person. We have all heard the saying, but knowledge is indeed POWER!

2. Have you had a career change? One that you always wanted?

If yes - your thoughts, beliefs and actions made the new job a reality. The universe responded to your thoughts and desires and literally performed miracles to bring you new opportunities, which in turn helped you to manifest your dream career!

This didn't happen by accident.

3. Are you driving the car you envisioned yourself in years ago?

Did you keep looking at pictures, posters, magazines or TV programmes that focused on this car?

You imagined this, you pictured yourself driving it, you **felt the feelings** of driving it and yes, you guessed it - YOU achieved it, by transforming those thoughts, feelings and visions into reality!

4. Did you go out in an outfit that you saw online and pictured yourself in? You loved it, you tried it on and you felt amazing!

When you feel and look amazing, you give off good energy and good energy creates MORE enjoyment (and more things to be grateful for).

5. Did you lose contact with someone that you wished to reconnect with?

Did you get yourself a mobile phone and a social media account, which enabled you to get back into contact with that old friend?

Maybe it's a friend that you couldn't imagine being without these days.

This all happened for a reason.

6. Did you pass those crucial exams that you were so worried about at the time?

Do you look back at those long, hard revision sessions and beam with pride at what an amazing achievement you now hold in your hands?

Did your results open up new career paths and new travel opportunities?

Did you enter into a new relationship as a result of new experiences and new contacts?

Well done YOU!

7. Are you loved-up with the partner of your dreams?

Are they everything you envisioned?

Your imagination and dreams aligned with real people and real events, to bring you both together.

8. Are you happy as Larry as you chill out in the comfort of your own home?

Do you look around you, at the aesthetically pleasing décor that YOU chose?

Do you beam with pride as you admire the colours, the furnishings, the finishing touches, the candles, the beautiful scents and the photos that surround you?

No doubt you had a vision in your mind for exactly how you wanted all of the rooms to be.

If you're anything like me, you may have had a favourites photo album on your phone, FULL of inspirational ideas for a long time before the ideas physically came to life.

Credit to YOU.

How amazing are our minds?!

Thoughts become things, so please remember to regularly acknowledge how far you have come and how amazing you can continually be.

Most importantly - ALWAYS remember to be your own best friend.

Be kind to yourself and practise self-love every single day.

Let's just look at these brief bullet points as healthy reminders of how unique you are and how you can be/become the person you will be forever proud of.

It is NEVER too late for self-improvement.

Show gratitude to yourself, show gratitude to your life and show gratitude to everything IN your life and in the words of Tears for Fears;

"Welcome to your life, there's no turning back..."

NEVER FORGET TO BE GRATEFUL.

Welcome to the **NEW** 'Magical World of YOU!'

Homework:

Just how proud of yourself are you?

Make a list of 10 things that make you beam with self-pride. The 10 items on your list can range from childhood achievements to recent achievements.

Elaborate on each milestone - explaining *why* you are so proud and how you *felt* when each event happened.

How did each event *change your life*?

1
_____

_____

_____

_____

2
_____

_____

_____

_____

3
_____

_____

_____

_____

4
_____

_____

_____

5
_____

_____

_____

6
_____

_____

_____

7
_____

_____

_____

8
_____

_____

_____

_____

9

_____

_____

_____

10

_____

_____

_____

Highlight anything that stands out for you in the following chapters.

This is YOUR book and you may wish to refer back to your favourite points when you have finished reading all of the chapters.

Re-read it all as many times as you need to (as a reminder of your own capabilities) because the more you read something, the more it sinks in.

CHAPTER 1

Mindset

To elaborate on my earlier point - how we think and what we believe, has a massive impact on how our days play out.

By maintaining a positive mindset, and by refusing to let negative thoughts, doubts, fear, guilt and habitual beliefs take over your mind, you can learn to count your blessings and move forward (without regret).

In simple terms, this is exactly what the Law of Attraction is all about! Some people may be more familiar with the following terms (rather than the LOA):

- The law of the universe.

- You reap what you sow.

- You get back what you give out.

- Karma.

- The power of prayer.

- Getting your comeuppance.

- Be careful what you wish for.

All of the above sayings are basically getting the same point across, so remember – always be kind and always look at unfortunate events as opportunities and lessons (rather than setbacks).

Whether people choose to accept it or not, we really do reap what we sow. It is down to YOU and you ONLY as to whether you choose to dwell on past events and wallow in self-pity,

OR...

Whether you pick yourself up and make some changes to improve your own life.

No one is going to do it all for you.

You have to take charge of your own life and work for what you want.

To reiterate - ANY dream is achievable if you BELIEVE... and in the words of Pablo Picasso:

"Everything you can imagine is real"

The world around us is literally shaped by what we are actually focusing our attention on.

Studies show that we can miss vital signs that are right in front of us when we are so engrossed in something else.

When you're fully focused on something, you are overlooking something else that may NEED your focus.

For example:

- If you are stressing about something while driving, you could easily miss a hazard.

- If you are so focused on work demands and this is encroaching on your home life, you could fail to recognise that another human or pet needs your help at home.

Remember to be present in the moment and treasure life's precious experiences.

Everyone is so busy these days, but did you know that we are not actually 'supposed' to multitask as much as we seem to always do nowadays?

We are meant to focus on one thing at a time, so that it is done properly and with intention.

Also, a healthy reminder for you;

We actually only work to our best abilities for a maximum of 90 minutes before we start to lose focus.

Ok so I'm not completely stuck in the 'Little House on the Prairie' bubble - I do agree that the creation of emails, instant chat and messenger app's help us to send/receive quick sharp answers, but again, a healthy work-life balance and staying connected to the natural world is key.

Embracing and stimulating our senses with time-out (away from work, phones, computers and social media) is vital for self-care, and for our sanity.

I personally believe that too much 'busyness' and multi-tasking in our lives is the main root of most anxieties.

Too many things going on at once and too many notifications flashing up on our phones = too many things whizzing around our brains at once.

- Personal emails,
- Work emails,
- Work stresses,
- Homelife stresses,
- Social media demands,
- Neighbours,
- Noisy traffic,
- Other outside noise,
- Phone calls,
- Hospital appointments,
- Meetings,
- To-do lists,
- Finances,
- Transport worries,
- Mealtimes,
- School demands,
- Homework,
- Outfit choices,

- Lots of conversations (all happening at once!)

The list goes on. It's all very exhausting!

The demands we face these days are literally ridiculous, so please remember to have TIME OUT from it all.

Including your phone.

A mistake that a lot of office workers and self-employed people may make, is checking work emails when it is their day off, or during 'out of office' hours.

This has become all too easy with the introduction of email apps and the popularity of working from home.

Everything is now at your fingertips.

I have done it myself many times and I strongly advise that (whatever job role and job responsibilities you have) you stick to your 'out of office' hours and enjoy your free time!

Otherwise, if you are having a lovely day off, doing the things you love with the people you love, you could run the risk of ruining your mindset and ruining those precious moments.

This is because if you check your emails to find something that 'rubs you up the wrong way' or stresses you out, it will naturally play on your mind and the smile could very easily be wiped from your face.

Those that you are with on your day off could also be adversely affected if your mindset changes from positive and happy, to uptight and snappy!

All because of a work stress that should not even encroach on your fun ***non-work*** times.

If YOU are at risk of the above scenario, be careful and immediately take action to ensure your time is your own and that more self-care is implemented.

The boss, the work demands, and the clients can wait until you are back in work mode (unless there is an emergency of course).

The ones who cherish you most, need you at your best during their quality time with you.

If you are someone who dreads going back to their job and you are juggling too many work demands, be sure to create structure to your day and take the necessary breaks during your shift (to refresh and recoup).

Keep the following prompts in mind:

- If you can, only check emails at set times throughout the day (instead of having notifications going off continually).

- If you need quiet time, find a quiet spot to focus.

- If the pile of papers and the messy desk are your distraction, take a few minutes to address this, before working on your main project or task. Tidy space = tidy mind.

- If the noise coming in from the open window is distracting you, shut it.

- If the radio helps you to focus (or if it is another distraction) turn it on/off.

- If you procrastinate and 'put off' the same dreaded jobs that just don't go away, then tackle the worst tasks first (before the other easier jobs) to get them out of the way.

Homework:

What is your biggest distraction?

Think about this for a moment or two.

Write down 5 of your biggest distractions.

1
_____

2
_____

3
_____

4
_____

5
_____

What did you write?

Do you know what the REAL answer is for us all?

More so than our phones, kids, hobbies, finances, noise, stress etc?

Your own MIND is your biggest disturber!

Yes, that's right - your thoughts are your own serial distractors.

Scientific research has proven this.

So blame other factors in your life as much as you want.

Moan about others to your heart's content if you wish, but the *reality* is that we are constantly disturbing ourselves with or own negative or doubtful thoughts.

And you can put a stop to this!

You may have those worries in the back of your mind that just keep niggling away at you, but the easy answer here is to just deal with the worries.

Tackle them head-on so that the weight can be lifted from your shoulders, and you can move on.

If it is something that is completely out of your control, then just laugh it off and BE HAPPY!

Do not waste precious energy worrying or stressing about factors that are out of your hands.

No matter what inventions, gadgets, money, investments, routines or therapies you have in your life, they can't 'fix' all of your own distractions.

It all comes down to YOU.

Acceptance, quiet time, reflection, meditation and rewiring your brain to not dwell on the negatives are all very important things to remember.

Just be happy in the moment.... No matter what the scenario.

This is exactly why taking a moment to silence the mind and stop it from wandering in the wrong direction is so valuable – this should be a daily practice.

Meditation and quiet time is important for adults, but it also helps the children of today too, as they have so much more going on for them these days than we used to.

I often just wish life would slow down for the little cherubs to be honest, as lots of noise and lots of demands too early-on must be so stressful for them...

And they should not even know what the word stress is as kids!

What a worry.

Maybe this is why more younger people struggle to deal with life's pressures these days.

We must help make the world a better place for our children, for our friends, for families and for our colleagues.

We need to make their days as bright and as positive as we can.

Therefore, if we see someone struggling with pressure, we should help in any way possible, to avoid escalation.

With such an increase in life pressures, I think it is more important than ever that everyone practises self-care.

On the other hand, I also think it's important that people are not too quick to get a GP diagnosis and a prescriptive drug for common ailments and common complaints (without actually assessing their own mindset and lifestyle first).

Rising concerns like anxiety, stress and depression can often be alleviated with the following:

- Nature and fresh air,
- Exercise,
- Healthy and natural food and drink,
- Natural remedies and therapies,
- Talking it out with someone (anyone),
- Controlling our own minds,

- Calming music,

- Happy/upbeat music,

- Taking regular time-out,

- Breathing slowly and deeply,

- Making positive changes,

- Company,

- Doing something you enjoy.

The aim of the tools in this book is to help bring it all back together again - for us all.

As I have already said - slowing down, mindful breathing and nature are some of the best natural remedies we can prescribe ourselves.

Prescription drugs can of course be amazing and positively life-changing, but we also need to be careful not to unknowingly create drug addictions that may not be entirely necessary for the ones taking them.

Also - don't just accept prescription drugs that simply act as a mask to the problem (rather than fixing the underlying issue) without making the important lifestyle and mindset changes listed in this book.

Low emotions come about for us ALL and some are completely unavoidable.

We do, however need to mindful of how often we are feeling low.

If you find yourself experiencing these overwhelming emotions or unease TOO often, (without a rational explanation) then get some professional advice as soon as you can.

Don't put it off.

The professionals are out there for a reason – to help make us feel better and happier.

If you are dismissed as being 'fine', but things do not get better for you, do not be afraid to GO BACK to your GP/other professional figure and ask to be assessed again.

If you know in your heart that you need therapy or an alternative remedy, please don't settle for being shown the door - until you get the help you need.

Everyone is an individual and there is no 'one size fits all' improvement plan.

Do your research of alternative therapies too and use your own **safe** 'trial and error' methods.

CHAPTER 2

The Young Brain

Ok, so to keep you on your toes, this chapter starts with a task!

Grab your best pen and think about the following:

Homework

Describe teenagers in 5 words.

Don't think about it for too long, just be honest with yourself (and me) and write down the FIRST 5 words that pop into your head.

1 _____

2 _____

3 _____

4 _____

5 _____

Now then, did you do what I think you *may* have done?

Did you judge and generalise?!

Be honest – did you *maybe* say any of the following?

- Stubborn,

- Lazy,

- Annoying,

- Argumentative,

- Cheeky,

- Irritable,

- Hormonal?

If so, you have already (unintentionally) labelled them and written off lots of amazing teenagers as 'just another teenager going through puberty'.

How about considering the following answers next time?

- Bright,

- Alert,

- Motivated,

- Misunderstood,

- Independent,

- Resilient,

- Unique,

- Ambitious,

- Creative,

- Bold,

- Confident.

Remember – we were all kids, and we were all teenagers – however long ago it may be!

Think about it – isn't it disheartening how so many parents, guardians, neighbours, teachers and strangers can just outright blame puberty for a teen's behaviour.

It's crazy that we do this.

If said teen is being creative and trying new things, we should not dampen their freedom and their ideas as 'just a phase'. We should fully embrace their uniqueness (not discourage them from setting their personality free).

Compressing it all just makes their childhood fun even more limited (and brings about their boring, perpetual adult life sooner)!

Remember that rationality does not even develop until they are much older, so we shouldn't expect too much from our kids and teens.

Cut them a bit of slack.

In fact, the transformation from gray matter to white matter in the brain doesn't actually complete until we are 25, meaning we are not actually a mature adult until the age of 25.

Not 18 or 21 as you may have originally thought.

This explains a lot I hear you say!

So be careful when raising and/or influencing teenagers. During these vital years, they can often feel like the world is watching and judging them.

The 'all eyes on you' feeling is so much more heightened at this point in life and it doesn't take a lot to knock someone's confidence.

We must big them up constantly, encourage confidence and tell them not to care about what others think.

We need to raise our kids right. They only get one childhood.

The children of the future could change the world for the better if there is more kindness and more happiness to go around.

So in the words of Michael Jackson:

"I'm starting with the man in the mirror... I'm asking him to change his ways, and no message could've been any clearer - if you wanna make the world a better place, take a look at yourself and make a change".

So why do we lose our sense of fun and imagination as we become adults?

Where does the innocence and the exciting magic go?

One reason why things are not as exciting as we age, is that our dopamine levels are higher as kids, compared to when we are fully fledged adults!

Also - as we grow, so do the layers that mould our personalities.

We start to be become affected by:

- The people we are surrounded by,

- The lessons we are taught in school,

- The places we see,

- The things we experience,

- The words we hear,

- The emotions we feel.

Peer groups have a big influence over youngsters.

Kids' brains are more malleable and so they can be moulded and influenced very easily. This is why we should be mindful of the words we use around children.

I recently walked past a dad saying to his child

"You're as thick as 2 short planks you are!"

Whether this was a joke or not, it didn't half rub me up the wrong way. I know that words have conviction and children are like sponges.

Children could very easily hear those words and believe them to be true.

Our words, energy and actions around children mould their entire world…. Their entire future.

LITERALLY.

Fill their conversations and experiences with magic and laughter. All in the interest of their wellbeing, positive mindset and, of course - a happy world for their future.

When we are young, we can believe in our own powers more, so we can build on our imagination. As kids, we also dare to ask the questions that we all want the answers to.

As adults, we must ensure we still have the ingredients and a good recipe to live our best lives.

When you do find those missing pieces to your own puzzle, keep them and keep that magic alive!

As we age, we get more set in our ways and it then becomes harder to manipulate and change that mould - because of engrained knowledge and old habits/beliefs.

Our brains also have a 'use it or lose it' function, but experiences and challenges do still continually strengthen and develop our brains.

No matter what our age.

This is why I love to revisit another particular childhood memory (playing Tetris!)

I used to play this on my brother's Gameboy when I was a kid and it is SUCH a good brain exercise for everyone.

We are often told these days to "be yourself" or "embrace your uniqueness" but unfortunately, the world today can be cruel.

Smallminded or uneducated people may like to insult those that are different to them and unfortunately, we can't always make people see that they are doing something wrong or 'unkind'.

This could be down to deep-routed conditioning. This, as we are learning through our own individual lives, takes a lot of effort to address.

This poses the question:

Can people really change?

Tell me - have you ever done one of those online personality questionnaires?

If your answer is no, do NOT bother.

What a load of rubbish! (In my opinion!)

You simply cannot base your life and your personality around a few generic questions alone.

My advice is to not label yourself or put yourself in these personality 'boxes' because of an online robot.

Some common labels that I often hear thrown around at people lately are:

- Shy and retiring,

- Quiet,

- Average,

- Reserved,

- Role Model,

- Self-centred,

- Warrior,

- Narcissistic,

- OCD,

- Modest,

- Confident,

- Impulsive,

- Introvert,

- Extrovert,

- Empath,

- Neurotic,

- Irrational,

- Rational.

One major factor that affects the reliability of these online questionnaire results is HONESTY!

Dishonesty when answering questions will throw out all of these methods of 'finding everyone's personality type'.

I mean, do you really think everyone gives completely honest answers to every question they are asked?

Such questionnaires don't even take into account everything else in that person's life, like:

- Core values,

- Lifestyle,

- Past and present life events,

- Current mindset,

- Genetic makeup,

- Nature,

- Nurture.

As we learn something new (like when we read a book and take in the new knowledge) we can invest in this knowledge and we can create new neuron pathways... and therefore create new ways of life.

There's always room for development, but as the brain hardens (the older we get) it does take more time, effort and consistency to train the brain new ways of thinking and new positive mindsets – hence regularly practising gratitude and LOA until it *does* become a daily habit.

I therefore urge you to ACT like the person you want to be.

Little by little... take baby steps to **feel** like, **look** like and **act** like the best version of you.

The YOU that is living their best life, with everything you wished for.... and it **will** become reality.

Homework

Have you ever stopped to ask yourself the following question?

Think about it and answer below.

Why are you on this planet?

_____

_____

_____

_____

_____

Embrace your superpowers, get rid of the distractions and show off your skills.

Master your own mind and be your own sunshine!

CHAPTER 3

Blessings

Don't worry, I'm not getting all biblical on you here... But knowing how blessed you are is the very foundation for building your dream life.

Health, love and happiness are amongst our top blessings, and you can improve ANY other aspect of your life too (love, career, travel, body image, fitness, financial status etc), providing you commit to doing so with focus and drive.

Now then.... Although we want to achieve and tick off all our bucket lists and dreams, I must add that you simply cannot expect to achieve **big** things if you are not grateful for all of the **small** (but VERY significant) things that you already have!

It is therefore very important that you see how lucky and blessed you already are, to even be comfortable and capable right at this very second!

Let's look at some wonders of the world that are at our fingertips every single day:

- **Breathing** is an amazing blessing!

You are alive and taking in the luscious air around you!

I can't stress enough how invigorating it is being amongst the great outdoors and taking in the sights, sounds and smells.

If you are indoors right now, take a deep, meaningful breath and see how amazing you actually feel as you breathe out with a grateful smile.

- Reading this book is a blessing, as you have the **education** to read and understand the words in front of you. Some people are not even fortunate enough to be able to read.

- Drinking clean, healthy **water** is a blessing – one that people take for granted.

To have running water at your disposal is a true luxury.

Your body is made up of water, so each and every precious cell in your body needs water to thrive and stay healthy.

- Having access to good **food** is a blessing.

Eating at home, dining out in fancy restaurants or embracing the 'grab and go' sections of your local shop are all blessings.

Some people would give anything to simply have access to safe and edible food, never mind having the freedom to choose exactly what they can devour at the first hint of hunger.

- The **sunrise** and the **sunset**.

They mark beginning and end of each day.

We can cram so much happiness, joy and fun in every single day. It's up to YOU how you spend each day from hereon.

- Your good **health** is your greatest blessing.

Being in good health and being grateful for your amazing, fully-functioning body is one of the most vital wake-up calls you can possibly have.

Some people (a lot of people, unfortunately) take their health for granted every day and don't actually realise the importance of good health until their own health is compromised.

Taking our bodies for granted needs to stop - ***right now***.

Be grateful for your health **NOW** and look after yourself and your whole body every single day (as a priority).

Without health, we literally have nothing.

Homework:

Take a moment to stand or sit in a comfy spot outside – (preferably in nature)

Close your eyes and take some *slow,* deep breaths.

Silence your mind.

While breathing in that lovely fresh air, express your gratitude for this luxury.

Think only happy thoughts.

Take yourself back to your favourite memory (or forward to your dream location).

Smile while you do this!

Feel your whole body benefiting from the oxygen that you are feeding it.

If you fancy it, add in a cheeky little bodily stretch while you're doing this.

As you breathe and stretch, think about each limb, each marking on your skin and each function in your body.

Thank God/the Universe for blessing you with your miraculous body, your beautiful unique skin and your perfect health.

Give thanks for the amazing day ahead.

Do this for as long as you wish.

Don't rush when you decide to stand back up to go back indoors.

Lift yourself calmly and safely.

...Guess what?! You just MEDITATED!

'Another dodgy word' do I hear you say?

Well, if monks and humming spring to mind at this point, please bear with me for the next chapter.

CHAPTER 4

Meditation

Meditating is literally just:

- Calming yourself down,

- Breathing correctly,

- Getting comfortable,

- Clearing the chaos from your mind,

- Replacing the chaos with calm, peace and happiness,

- Enjoying the **NOW.**

It is as simple as that!

Granted, there is a lot more to it for those that eat, sleep, breathe and **live** meditation as a way of life, but what I am trying to get across, is that meditation/therapy/a period of reflection/whatever you wish to call it, is important and beneficial for each and every one of us.

Practising meditation can work wonders for you and everyone around you.

Each individual person in this world has different interests, different triggers, different ideals and different lives (reiterating what I said earlier about how no one else is YOU), so you can tailor your meditative journey to your own wants and needs.

- Some people like to do Yoga or Pilates on set days and times to find their calm.

- Some like to meditate solely on their own. This may be on their lunch break, on the train, tram, tube or bus.

You can still meditate in the presence of external noise, but you may choose to use earphones or a headset to quieten any unwanted sounds while you concentrate.

- Some people like to do it in groups, as a social gathering.

- Some people make a point of practising meditation amongst the trees, while being at one with nature.

- Some may attend local forest bathing sessions, to meet new people at the same time.

- Some may soak in their own cosy bath with a motivational podcast and a beverage of their choice.

My choice of meditation is going on a beautiful horse ride with friends (or solo).

I love taking in the views and breathing in the fresh countryside air, while listening to the birds sing.

The adrenalin-boosting canters and gallops, combined with the steady, chilled-out walks and trots (all while passing hikers, bikers and dog walkers) is peace and tranquillity to me.

I ride with a smile on my face. It makes me happy, so my happiness shines through my eyes, my smile and my body.

I do many other things that I know make me happy, as this recipe is definitely one that satisfies my fulfilment pallet:

Happy + Fulfilled = Healthy.

Make sure happiness is on your own daily menu.

I am sure you are aware of the importance of 'happy hormones' so go find your own happiness and reap the rewards.

Be happy as often as you possibly can be.

Make smiling your priority and I promise you - your future self will be forever grateful you did.

So.... When working on your goals, aspirations, bucket lists and to-do lists, be sure to get a clear plan - both in your mind and on paper.

Envision having it all, so that the universe has a clear instruction of what to grant you.

One tool that is rather popular when manifesting dreams to reality is the 'ol' faithful' vision board.

I have an old vision board in my bedroom, and do you know what? I hadn't actually looked at it for a while... until the other day!

I was blown away by the amount of photos (that were originally pinned to my vision board as 'just' dreams) that are now in my life as my true reality!

I was literally smiling my socks off at it and feeling VERY grateful while looking through my chosen pic's.

Seeing how much the universe and I have made these things reality is phenomenal.

I am literally living my dreams.

This is proof that the more you:

- See,

- Visualise,

- Believe,

- Feel,

- Work towards, and

- Daydream about the things you want, the harder the universe will work to make it all happen for you.

The universe needs your belief and your clear vision, to be able to move mountains for you.

Good feelings, good vibrations and good energy will make it all happen quicker than you may think.

My vision board items didn't all come to life right away. Some did indeed show up very quickly, others have taken years, and some are still on the horizon, but I KNOW that more of my biggest dreams and achievements are yet to come.

It's all about keeping the faith and believing in yourself.

Homework:

Make (or buy) a large vision board of your own.

Mine is a corkboard from my local homeware store, but you can use card, canvas, or anything else that you think could do the job.

Fill your vision board up with pictures of all your dreams/wants/ambitions.

There are so many free photo apps around these days, that there is no excuse for not doing this task.

The way I did it, was to save screenshots (or real pics of my own) in my favourites album on my phone. This way, it was easier to just select them all together in bulk for printing.

Your vision board can include things like:

- Your dream house,

- Lots of money,

- Your ideal job,

- Your dream holiday,

- Perfect health,

- Your dream body,

- Meal ideas.

- A pet that you long for.

- The perfect partner,

- A baby,

- A car,

- A pair of designer shoes.

Whatever your own personal goals are, make it a reflection of YOU.

The vision board doesn't have to be full of photos alone, you can pin material, jewellery, gadgets (or anything you like to it!)

Once you have everything in place and you are happy with it, you will need to place it in an area of your home that you continually visit.

You could try your kitchen, bedroom, bathroom, or anywhere that you feel it will be seen the most (by YOU!)

Seeing all of your dreams regularly in your mind, your home, in photos and while daydreaming and meditating, will create more manifesting impact.

I remember putting a picture of lots of £50 notes on my phone's screensaver/wallpaper - in the hope that I manifest more money. I now see endless £50 notes all the time!

Try it all for yourself and prepare to be dazzled by the limitless possibilities that surround you.

CHAPTER 5

I Don't Have the Time!

Ok, so I bet some of you will be thinking:

"But I don't have the time for hobbies" or

"There's not enough hours in the day for me to add something else to the list"

Well I'm sorry, but that's just BULL.

This type of obstructive reaction is the very reason your life may not be moving in the direction you want it to.

You are your own resistance!

MAKE... THE... TIME!

There are 24 hours in every day.

If you feel you don't have enough time to yourself, get up earlier in the mornings.

Start your day earlier.

Rise and shine my friend! Rise and shine!

A quick example;

- I have always worked full time,
- I have studied very hard for many years of my life (around my work)
- I have a husband, a son and a dog at home,
- I have amazing family members and friends to see and enjoy,
- I have hobbies to embrace,
- I volunteer for a charity that I am passionate about,

- I need to 'fit in' self-care,

- I ride and look after a horse,

- I am writing a book,

- Blah blah blah.

'All' of this, and I still make time to work on my dreams and goals (and my own responsibilities are no doubt, ***nothing*** compared to all the amazing, busy-bee Superheroes out there!)

What I want to make clear (at the risk of peeing the majority of my readers off) is that there are too many couples or individuals who constantly whinge about their life/family/job/neighbours/friends/household chores/lack of money.

They are constantly on a downer or acting like the world owes them a favour.

They act as though others are so privileged, and they are not... which results in grudges being held, which in turn only makes their situation worse due to the bad energy they give off.

It's a vicious circle and this can create a downward spiral of unhappiness and bad health if not dealt with appropriately.

I call this kind of unfulfilled person a 'Negative Norace' or a 'Debbie Downer'.

I use these terms light-heartedly and of course never mean any disrespect when doing so.

I mention these names as a way to encourage self-love and kind words, rather than using insults or unkindness towards yourself and/or others.

We are all different, but let's just address the all too common 'mum guilt' for example.

For my mum readers, you may be very familiar with this term.

It could be that you felt guilt because you unintentionally:

- Missed your child's sports day,

- Turned your back for a second (and they bumped their head),

- Sent them to school without their PE kit,

- Broke a promise,

- Paid attention to one child more than the other,

- Couldn't afford to buy what they ask for.

The list goes on and on, but please remember that we are all human and we all make mistakes.

We cannot be perfect all the time, but what does truly matter is that love conquers all.

Love is the greatest gift you could ever possibly give to your child, so give yourself a break.

Leave the dishes and any other avoidable time-consuming stresses.

All of that can wait.

Kids grow up fast and precious memories are WAY more important than pretending you have to have a showroom 24/7.

I always say that a messy, **happy** family home is far more important for the wellbeing of our children, than fretting over misplaced items, ironing and washing.

Just be present, happy and grateful as you look around your home at life's great wonders (and those wonders include the mess, the mountain of toys and the soiled clothes, because they are **WORTH IT!**)

Let's engrain freedom, confidence, FUN and self-belief into the children of today, so that they carry this with them throughout their whole lives.

Make more time for the important things in life and spend less time on the things that don't really matter.

Be present in the moment and be FUN.

The following task is an extension of a little tool I came up with when I was a College Lecturer. I used it to lighten the mood, and to make my students believe in themselves.

During tense times like exams or assessments, I would say "Hey you, I'll have no negativity here thank you" every time my students said something along the lines of:

"I can't do it"

"I'm not good enough"

"I'm never going to pass this course"

I would say "Right, put a pound in that Negative Nancy pot please!"

There was never actually a physical Negative Nancy pot there, but it made them stop to think about their own self sabotage... and sure enough, they all came through and passed their studies.

Homework

Get a jar, a bottle or a pot of your choice. Decorate it and write a personalised title on it.

The title can be anything along the lines of:

"No Negativity Here!"

"Words that hold me back!"

"Things to let go of!"

"Negative Nancy Jar"

"Positivity Vibes ONLY Jar"

The choice is yours, but I suggest that you use a money pot (where you chuck a pound in each time you label yourself or others with a negative word).

This could end up being a nice little earner when it comes to opening it up!

You can look at this as a reminder to big yourself up each time you accidently choose negativity instead of positivity.

If you prefer, here is another option (instead of/as well as the money pot)

If you are currently stuck in the habit of using words like:

"I can't"

"I hate"

"I'm worried"

Stop yourself, write the words down on scrap paper and chuck them away (into the jar).

This jar may stick around for years and when you finally open it up, you will do so with such pride at how far you have come since then!

This option makes you more mindful of your daily word choices.

As you replace negative words with more positive words, positivity will become second nature, which of course raises your vibrations and makes your world a better place.

Both of these options are great for any children in your life too.

CHAPTER 6

Finding Your Happiness

If you find it hard to identify your happy place, your favourite hobbies or interests, or if you tend not to try new things, then hopefully the following basic tools will help.

Whatever people choose to do for enjoyment, it is THEIR own therapy.

Don't follow the crowd, find your own happiness boosters.

As we know, everyone is different, so be sure to never, ever make fun of people for their chosen paths, as their hobbies and passions are reflections of their own happiness.

Everyone has the right to make their own decisions, and for many people, these chosen hobbies or practises are often their own answers to relieving stress, anxiety or worry.

Find your solace.

Homework:

Write a list of **AT LEAST** 5 things that made you smile today.

1
_____

2
_____

3
_____

4 _____

_____

5 _____

_____

I find that having a pretty pen and a cup of tea always motivates me when making gratitude lists or journaling - simply because it's nice to look at something aesthetically pleasing while building your dream life!

If you struggled to think of things that made you smile today, I'll help you out with my own:

1. My British Bulldog, Mavis has been snoring and trumping next to me (the whole time I have been typing). This has kept a smile on my face.

2. The smile on my beautiful son's face this morning when he woke up and came into our room.

3. The birds feeding and singing on the table outside my window.

4. Looking at pictures on my phone from our fun weekend. I LOVE photo memories.

5. The beautiful flowers in the vase that I am gazing over at.

Now had today been a typical work day, I would have a lot more things to add to the list.

I would have driven to work and smiled with people all day, but as I have had a productive day on my own, the smile-jerkers are confined to my home space - on this occasion!

Some other things that regularly make me smile though are:

• Other smiley people who pass me by in the street. Smiling back at one another spreads more good energy, positivity and light.

- Seeing children laughing and playing is an amazing joy-spreader. It always makes me happy when I see happy lil munchkins.

- Seeing people cuddle their family, friends or partners makes my heart smile.

- Seeing thriving wildlife on my walks always makes me smile.

- Christmas! Just the word Christmas and all the magic associated with Christmas makes me VERY giddy.

So how many have you done? Just the 5? Or have you smiled a 100 times today?! I'm sure you have if you really think about it... and if not, **go**, **do** or **see** something that DOES make you smile!

Immediately!

Go on you little rascal.

Are you smiling yet?!

Please make it your daily priority to list all of the things that made you smile each day.

You could even take it one step further and do exactly as me and my own family do each evening:

Gratitude Tokens!

Teaching kids valuable life lessons is a great way to ensure their happiness and fulfilment – both during their youthful years and well into their adult life.

Dreams, wishes, magic and fun are forever alive in my home.

Childhood magic must never die. It is what makes life amazing and also means that children can believe in themselves and their own abilities.

We must never, ever dull their shine or dampen their dreams.

Now don't be fooled – life isn't ALWAYS about fairy dust, smiles and paradise in my home.

We have our fair share of tantrums, crossed words, discipline reinforcement and 'off days' in our house.

The key is (again) to have that healthy balance.

We have to ensure that priorities are met and that boundaries are set.

Everyone parents their own way with their own kids, and that is the choice of each individual parent or guardian, but one thing should always be consistent:

Life should be absolutely amazing!

Everyone should choose happiness, but there should also be barriers and the word 'NO' where needed.

As hard as it can be at times, growing children (and adults!) have to learn to accept **no** for an answer, in order to come to terms with life's future lessons.

I implemented our little gratitude token ritual a couple of years ago and it has proven a daily success for us all.

I cut out some tokens (just colourful card shapes).

One was a green tree, one was an orange circle, one was a gold star and one was a glittery triangle.

Token 1 stated "Top 3 things you are most grateful for, from today"

Token 2 stated "What are you most proud of yourself for, from today?"

Token 3 stated "What could you have maybe improved on/done better today?"

Token 4 stated "List your top 3 wishes and dreams"

The 3 of us do these every single night before bed. We listen to each other, praise each other and support each other when chatting about our answers.

I find that it is a great reflection tool, one that makes us appreciate the events of the day, and one that also makes us think about any areas of improvement there may be.

We have already seen many of our own wishes & dreams come true since doing these tokens and the beauty of them is that you can swap and change your dreams & wishes as you see fit!

Words have power.

Written words (repeated often) have even more power!

Homework:

Try it for yourself!

Make your own gratitude tokens.

Choose your design and/or words to reflect our own uniqueness and start them today.

Happy wishing!

CHAPTER 7

Energy

What is energy?

I don't mean the kind of energy that makes us hyper and bounce around everywhere after too many skittles.

I mean the vital life energy that we can't see. The energy that keeps us in check and the energy that also keeps us alive.

This same energy is constantly providing signs, lessons and intuition to us.

When I talk about people having good or bad energy, I am referring to how a person makes you feel.

Do you ever meet someone and instantly take a liking to them?

Do you think "Wow, I am so glad I met this person"?

If you feel that someone is awesome, you want to spend more time with them as they make you feel **good.**

On the other hand, do you ever walk into a room and are overcome with a feeling of unease?

Was there someone that made you feel anxious and you couldn't quite put your finger on it?

Maybe the body language was off-putting, or maybe their tone of voice was abrupt or stand-offish?

If you work for a large corporate company and regularly attend board meetings, then you may agree that someone's energy (or vibe) can potentially be the difference between a good meeting and a bad meeting.

A good end-result, or a disappointing end-result.

This same energy, whether it's your own, or someone else's, can be the difference between having a good day or a bad day!

If you wake up in a bad mood and stomp around with a negative vibe, you could ruin the whole chain of events for the day ahead. For yourself AND others!

Literally – I could not be speaking truer words.

The way to flip the switch and ensure that your meetings, days, weeks, months and years go swimmingly, is to change that mindset from negative and miserable, to positive and grateful.

Now I'm not saying that we won't have any issues or deflating obstacles along the journey of life, but how we now choose to DEAL with what is thrown our way is the deciding factor in whether we live a happy, enjoyable life, or a dark and faithless life.

Take a look at your life and the people in it.

Do you surround yourself with life's angels? Or do you constantly seem to hang onto life's energy suckers?

Toxic relationships, bitter people and anyone that does not bring out the best in you need to be reviewed.

Take a mental note of your feelings and your state of mind when you are around certain people.

If you find that you get anxious, uneasy, panicky, angry or tense whenever you are around a certain someone, you need to come to the realisation that this person is probably not the best person for you... and that is ok!

Not everyone is suitable for everyone, and sometimes we outgrow people too.

It's ok to not 'click' with someone, but it's also very important to realise this.

Instead of making each other's lives uncomfortable, you just need to respectfully cut (or limit) contact with those types of people (if possible).

I do however understand that cutting ties may not always be possible – especially if it is someone you work with in close proximity!

It could even be a family member, friend, roommate or other acquaintance that you have to see often.

My advice, (if you find yourself in this scenario) is to always smile, be polite and respectful and only engage in conversations that serve you and your work/ home environment.

Making each other's lives more difficult through bitterness will only increase negative feelings and negative actions, which will just come back on you.

Remember – what you give out comes back to you, so always be the bigger, better (and happier) you.

If they bring nothing to your table, kick them to the curb.

I now cut out anything, or anyone that does not bring good energy to my life.

It is **absolutely necessary** to go with your gut feeling on things.

If something doesn't feel right, someone or something makes you feel on edge, anxious or worried, just move away.

Did you know that external factors in our lives can affect our internal bodily functions?

Stress, worry and depression can all manifest as physical and very real internal health issues.

This is exactly why it is very important to listen to your body, take note of your gut feelings and make positive changes, both in, and around your own body.

Why do you think people:

- Become sick with worry?

- Shaky with nerves?

- Or their bowel movements are all over the place when they are going through something significant?

Because our gut health plays a major part in the state of our health and wellbeing! Our gut is like our second brain.

- Lessen the bad feelings and the bad experiences.

- Increase the good feelings and the good experiences.

Your body and soul will be thankful when you do!

Homework

1. List all the things/people/experiences that bring fulfilment, joy and smiles to your life.

With each smile-jerker that you list, expand on WHY they bring you joy, and how they make YOU feel when you are around them.

Writing and thinking about your good feelings increases your good vibrations and in turn, prolongs your feelings of happiness and makes your life instantly better.

_____

_____

_____

_____

_____

_____

2. Now list all the things/people/experiences that make you feel sad, down, depressed, stressed or uneasy.

We don't want to linger on these ones, but noting them down recognises, acknowledges and accepts them for what they are.

This way, you are not trying to cover up or totally mask these feelings by pretending that life is 100% perfect all of the time.

_____

_____

_____

_____

_____

You can now start to assess how you feel in certain situations and begin consciously reducing these undesirable feelings.

This will happen naturally by limiting negative interactions and reacting in a more positive way to them when you do encounter such feelings.

Doing all of this allows the negative feelings to pass much quicker, so the more mindful you are of this process, the more you will start to notice that your low moments don't hang around as long as you would have previously let them.

Simply replace the negative feeling with a happy feeling by turning your brain's focus to your happy thoughts instead.

Hello Happy Place!

This process will tip the scales.

As long as you are simply in a positive state of mind more than you are in a negative state of mind, I promise this will change your life forever.

CHAPTER 8

Mother Nature

If you still find it hard to grasp the concept of good and bad energy, or that every person or thing vibrates, then let's look at the wonderful world of nature.

- Water vibrates, and hopefully we all agree that water is magical, vital for life, and healing.

Drinking water helps to boost our energy, it feeds our cells and helps to flush out toxins.

- Plants and trees vibrate, and they provide us with oxygen and LIFE!

Walking amongst trees produces wonderful energy, vibrance and happy hormones.

Trees stand tall and continually go through the seasons and changes each year.

They can get bashed about in the wind and rain and yet they still never fail to flower when the warmer seasons come back around.

We humans can learn a lot from these powerful living beings.

Walking with, sitting next to, or hugging trees connects us to nature and literally revives our bodies and souls.

- Without bumblebees, there would be no pollination for crops, fruit and veg.

The entire ecosystem would suffer and the whole rippling effect on the planet could eventually result in the collapse of human life!

- Without mushrooms (fungi) to aid in forest decomposition, there would be no new plant or insect life!

They are vital for other well-known food-making processes, like those involved in winemaking, bread-making, beer-making and cheese-making.

Have you ever noticed old rotting food on a bird feeder? You may have said "Eeeew!" at the fungi growing on it, but if you go back days later, the fungi will be gone and new life/new grass will have grown in its place!

Wow!

- Without butterflies, the rest of nature would suffer.

The 'Butterfly Effect', in simple terms is when the slightest atmospheric change can lead to unpredictable (and sometimes majorly significant) events across the world!

Get the picture?

All life is connected – from each individual cell, to full-grown humans, trees, mammals, feelings and relationships.

Energy (or vibrations) should always be good, to encourage a happy world with amazing outcomes, as opposed to bad vibrations causing unwanted occurrences and events.

We ALL have a part to play.

As the legendary Beach Boys song goes, when someTHING or someONE gives you good vibrations, you feel great and great things happen!

"I, I love the colourful clothes she wears… and the way the sunlight plays upon her hair.

I hear the sound of a gentle word… on the wind that lifts her perfume through the air.

I'm pickin' up good vibrations, she's giving me the excitations.."

Good vibes are a sign from the universe that things are going well. That you are on the right path.

Likewise, if things or people feel 'off' to you, then it's a sure sign to walk away and remove yourself from that unnerving situation.

If you haven't heard this song ('Good Vibrations') please play it right now! It has **such** an amazing feel-good vibe.

Homework

What amazing gifts do YOU have?

Dig deep for the big and the small – you have many.

I want you to expand on how your gifts, talents and good traits come in handy to help both yourself, and others.

If you struggle to list 10 things, ask your nearest and dearest for answers.

Remember your worth!

1 _____

_____

_____

2 _____

_____

_____

3 _____

_____

_____

4 _____

_____

_____

5 _____

_____

_____

6 _____

_____

7 _____

_____

_____

8 _____

_____

_____

9 _____

_____

_____

10 _____

_____

_____

CHAPTER 9

Dealing with Rejection

Never, ever pursue something purely because of peer pressure, family pressure, or because you simply feel you HAVE to.

Whatever you choose to do in life, should always be what YOU truly want to do.

Remember that the universe speaks to us in lots of different ways, so each time you feel:

- Rejected,

- Lost,

- Disappointed,

- At a loss,

- Upset,

- Angry that something didn't work out... just know that something even better is in store for you and your future.

Understandably, many people follow in their family's footsteps and mirror the line of work their parent(s) had, and this is absolutely wonderful... as long as you enjoy it!

I feel that not following your own dreams and not going with what is truly in your heart, only prolongs the inevitable (disappointment and unfulfillment further down the line).

You will no doubt go through many different jobs, friends, partners and experiences to get to where you are meant to be.

There will be ups and downs along the way, but always remember that YOU are destined for big things.

If life was a perfectly straight road, we would not learn the lessons that need to be taught.

The unpredictable twists, turns, speedbumps and emotions make things exciting.

They also pinch us and remind us to be aware of flaws, opportunities, mistakes, consequences and betrayal.

We learn from both bad experiences and good experiences, so that we can better deal with life's obstacles in the future.

Long story short, I have predominantly worked in management and lecturer roles, but I did **many** different jobs beforehand.

Some examples of the different career steppingstones I have bounced along (in no particular order) are:

- Bar work,
- Telesales,
- Reception,
- Compliance,
- PA,
- Owner (2 x beauty salons),
- Phlebotomist,
- Beauty Therapist,
- Medical Aesthetician,
- Makeup Artist,
- Nail Technician,
- Chinese Medicine,
- Marketing,

- Sales,

- Qualification Assessor,

- Legal Advisor,

- IQA,

- Customer Service,

- L&D Business Partner,

- Business Development,

- Finance...

And so on.

Over the years, I have worked very hard to prove myself.

My senior roles were gained through lots of hard work, lots of qualifications and lots of experience.

What I will always remember though, is that all of my previous jobs played important roles in my life's paths.

I enjoyed (and still do) all aspects of training in my chosen career, so the fact that I love my work so much (and don't see it as a chore) makes all the difference.

Over the years, I have travelled to many different parts of the UK and overseas with work. Enjoying new experiences and learning about different cultures, to me is amazing!

When I lost work (and money) through redundancies and loss of college funding, understandably I was angry, upset, gutted and disappointed.

I felt rejected and undervalued.

These feelings were ok at the time, as I just had to let all of the emotions out (inevitably!)

Once the low mood passed, I was then able to reassess my situation (when I was in a calmer, more rational state).

Turns out that further down the line, I had a much better career, with many more perks in store for me.

Isn't life intriguing?!

I stand by the fact (even more so these days) that everything happens for a reason.

All of the events in our lives lead us to where we need to be.

I would not be where I am now if all of the past events had not occurred and taught me the lessons I needed to learn.

So never regret anything from your past– whether it's studies at college, a bad relationship or a controversial choice you made – every single life experience and every episode of education serves a purpose in your life and your future.

Never say words such as "I wasted my life at that college/school/job/house" as those experiences needed to happen – to make you, YOU.

Therefore, no time is ***ever*** wasted time.

The people we have met along the way and the life chapters that have passed, make for great stories, great giggles, cringeworthy moments and heart-warming reminiscing with loved ones.

So... Remember to put number one first.

If you struggle to put yourself first in life, then think of yourself as a seal.

Picture it.

Amongst a whole colony of seals, you are all chilling on the rocks and a killer whale is approaching.

That whale is there to grab his meal. You simply cannot choose to just follow the crowd.

The others could get swallowed up in a flash if they follow the others and find themselves in a struggle.

YOU - the brave, independent seal who remains calm is the one that stays safe and sound. Your faith and trust in the universe will reign supreme... So choose life!

Make some daily changes. Take those little steps to be grateful and KIND.

When you are in a rush or having a stressful episode, don't use that as an excuse to disrespect the shopkeeper or the receptionist.

Smile at everyone.

Say good morning.

Brighten their day with kindness and appreciation.

The last thing they need is someone else giving them a hard time because you're in a bad mood.

Happiness spreads happiness but remember that bad moods can also be contagious!

Get into the habit of writing down all the little the perks of your day.

When I did this for the first time, I could not believe all of the little wins I'd had throughout that particular day alone.

Little wins lead to big wins!

- Be mindful,
- Journal,
- List your 'to do's',
- Be kind,
- Be ambitious,
- Respect others.

As all of these life tweaks come together, you can rediscover yourself again and enjoy each new day – all while watching your life improve miraculously.

Any new ideas that you have along the way – write them down, make plans and work on them!

Make your dreams reality and remember that all of the greatest inventors were/are normal people.

Creativity applies to everyone, and no two people have the exact same creative flair, which is why we all need to embrace our own individuality and invent our own unique goals.

Remember – we all like different music genres and new music is continually being made. We never run out of good songs, so whatever your life plans are, don't follow the herd – be your own production!

If you have those moments when you feel like you have hit a brick wall in terms of moving forward with your dreams (which we ALL do), you may need to reassess your surroundings again.

See if any of the following help you to feel inspired again:

- Have a nice soak in the bath.

I like to create a pretty, floral milk bath – with dimmed lights, crystals and candles.

I close my eyes, breathe deeply and slowly…. And enjoy the 'me time'.

If you don't have a bath, have an invigorating shower and try a cold blast at the end. This will certainly awaken and refresh your senses.

- Talk it out.

Tell your best friend that you are feeling out of sorts and need a bit of time-out with them. A good friendly chat and a giggle can make us feel much better.

- Embrace the elements.

Whatever the weather, take yourself on a nice walk and see if the fresh air and new sights make new ideas pop up for you.

- Have a tipsy tipple.

If you are partial to an alcoholic tipple, you may find that getting a little tipsy amongst loved ones can actually make you more insightful.

You may come up with a great new idea, discuss future opportunities and have that lightbulb moment where you find the missing piece to a puzzle!

- Get a good night's sleep.

We can often have those satisfying lightbulb moments after a good rest too, so get into bed early and let the creative subconscious mind take over while you dream.

- Daydream.

Daydreaming is great and **absolutely** necessary when manifesting your dreams to reality.

Your creativity seeds need regular attention and nurturing to grow. Otherwise, they are simply ideas without intention.

Homework

Start to journal (list/log) all of the things that you want to do in life.

These can be broken down into instant (or short-term) and long-term dreams.

Grab your best pen again and go ahead!

Include major 'bucket list' items, as these are your life goals, but also include things that you might currently refer to as 'chores' (you know - those things that you constantly procrastinate over).

I guarantee that words on paper are far more powerful and demanding than thoughts alone.

Putting pen to paper validates the words and creates an energy shift – pushing you closer to your goals.

When you tick off your list(s) as 'complete', you will feel happy and grateful that you took action to better your own life.

Getting things done results in satisfaction and self-pride.... Meaning even more self-love!

However big the dream or task, write it down.

The bigger your dreams, the better! And the more you get done and ticked off, the better.

You must believe that you deserve everything you want in life... and with belief, time, effort and patience...

You will achieve!

CHAPTER 10

Go Easy On Yourself

It's ok to not have it all figured out yet.

Once you do find your calling, you will know. Things will just click and natural actions will kick in.

I didn't know what I truly wanted to do straight from high school. I don't think many of us actually do, as we are so young when we finish school. We still have so much growing and maturing to do at this stage in our lives.

I got my GCSE's at school and my A-Levels at college, with the intention to go straight onto university (for another 4 years!) to become a secondary school English teacher.

By the end of my second year at college I had met new people and I decided that I wanted to get myself out there in the big wide world and start working. So I did!

Thank the Lord that I did!

I was earning and getting a taste of the real life (away from the regimented university education that I probably wouldn't have enjoyed anyway at that stage in my life).

This time-out helped me to find myself.

I was able to reflect on what actually interested me and I could then assess my future career choices in my own time.

Fast forward a couple of years or so, while a friend was doing my hair.

We were having one of those deep and meaningful conversations over a good wine (as you do!) and she said (while on the topic of jobs and careers) "why don't you study beauty, as you're so good with skincare and makeup?"

I took the advice of my friend and got my first Beauty Therapy Diploma in 2003.

This, of course led onto many more years of studying in the beauty and aesthetics industry.

As the years went on and my knowledge increased, I became more and more passionate about the advances of anti-ageing and human anatomy & physiology.

I soon decided that I DID want to become a teacher after all! Only not an English teacher, but a College Lecturer in my chosen profession.

I studied long and hard again, but this time achieving 2 valuable teaching qualifications and assessor awards.

All of this studying was done around my full time work, in addition to various other 'on the job' training (from admin, IT, sales and customer service courses, to the supervision and management training that led to my future managerial positions).

Working towards your dreams takes hard work, commitment and time.

You also need to choose a career that you are passionate about, because as I can now confirm – when you truly love your job and industry, you literally walk in and out of the workplace with a beaming smile and with a truly grateful heart.

CHAPTER 11

Memories

Have you ever noticed how revisiting places, smells and feelings can trigger vivid memories from the past?

These can even be memories from when you were a VERY young child!

Our bodies are amazing, miraculous works of art and are capable of so much more than we give them credit for.

If we smell something that takes us back to our younger days, it can trigger a lovely moment of nostalgia.

One that we can hopefully all relate to, is the smell of Pritt Stick or PVA glue from our school days.

I remember the massive plastic tubs of PVA glue that the Teacher would decant into our little stained plastic bowls for us all.

We would be given those cute lil plastic spatulas to go ahead spread it onto our creative masterpieces!

I also remember the satisfaction that came from peeling said glue from my fingers during lesson that afternoon.

We had those ancient wooden tables in our classrooms (with the pen marks and carvings all over them) and there would be lots of glue to peel off those too.

Ooh – while I'm on the subject, a couple more childhood memories for the ol' Olfactory System:

- The smell of marker pens.

- The smell of rubber from those traditional black pumps that we used to wear for P.E.

Wow, the smell of those elasticated fashion statements takes me right back.

- The smell of hospital.

I remember the smell of hospital so vividly and it always takes me back to those broken bones and stitches... Followed by pressies, sympathy and cuddles from my lovely Barney Bear.

Ahhhhhh, primary school days - those were the best days!

So the correct term for what I am talking about here is 'odour-evoked autobiographical memory'.

Memories that are linked to smells are often our strongest and most vivid memories, which are most commonly our earliest memories too (from when we were tiny kiddy winks!)

Any feelings or memories that make you happy, should ALWAYS be kept alive, as good thoughts and good energy make way for more good things.

Such memories may be your way of never letting go of a loved one, who has maybe since passed away. Remembering that person and how they made you feel during those good times, will make you happy that you had them in your life.

Holding onto great memories can be absolutely amazing and it is very pleasing to think back to the fun days.

For some people however, thinking back to past years may bring about undesirable feelings of sadness, loss, guilt, torture, abuse or lack.

Bad memories can have a habit of popping up and interrupting your day with unwanted negativity.

Are bad memories holding you back?

If so, you will need to address this issue if you want to achieve all of our goals and reach your full potential.

Thoughts become things and whatever we focus on or spend time on, will be the main occurrence in our lives.

For example - if you focus on happiness, fun, joy, excitement and abundance, you will forever be given more of these same things.

If you continually allow negative feelings to take over our mind, I'm afraid you will continually attract negativity.

This is the law of attraction.

The LOA is not some babble that someone decided to make up out of thin air. It is about scientific, factual life-lessons.

If you believe you will have a great day, your day will be amazing.

If you are a moaner, a whinger, and you always have your sob story to tell, you will forever be mediocre.

You will continue to be lacking, because you are repeatedly saying to yourself and others that you are lacking or 'hard done by'!

Whether you like to hear it or not….

- Focus on crap and your wish will be granted – you will undoubtedly receive more crappy experiences!

- Focus on every little thing that you are grateful and happy for, and your wish will be granted – you will receive more experiences that make you happy!

FACT!

Let me make this clear;

- Any bad feelings are negative. Bad feelings include jealousy, bitterness, worry, regret, fear, doubt, lack, sadness and hatred.

Please try your very best to stop these feelings from taking over your mind and send them on their way. This way, you can limit the amount of new 'bad' memories you create, and make more room for the great ones.

These feelings do not serve you, or those around you. Entertaining bad feelings will be detrimental to you and your own life.

- Any good feelings are positive – love, joy, happiness, pride, fulfilment, excitement, achievement, helpfulness and willingness to learn are all great feelings.

Flood your mind and your life with good feelings so that you can create endless new amazing memories.

Entertaining good feelings does indeed serve you, and those around you!

Spread joy, life and love!

CHAPTER 12

The World Today

Many people watch the mainstream news, with the majority audience probably feeling they get their daily dose of 'reality' from it.

I do not watch or read mainstream news.

People don't realise just how much our surroundings and senses affect our lives.

Lots of news content these days can be sad and/or negative, so if we are not careful, too much exposure to such content can unknowingly turn into a form of mind control that could end up making you fearful or depressed.

This is because it can consume too much of your time and energy, and even become addictive.

Turn the news off.

Tap into your senses.

SEE more beautiful visions... and less saddening visions.

- Watching the sun rise and set, for example (while truly being present, calm and patient in the moment) stimulates the senses like you wouldn't believe.

- Watching a live performance at the theatre awakens our senses and allows us to take in the amazing atmosphere that surrounds us.

Take note of the beautiful, grand historic building.

Look around at the chandeliers, the high ceilings, the artwork, the amazing musicians putting their hearts and souls into the beats and the melodies, the stage props, the costumes, the dancing and the mesmerising voices.

All of this (for me, personally) brings about an appreciation like no other.

HEAR more natural, beautiful, pleasing sounds... and less 'noise'.

- Some people have a TV on in the background at all times.

They have this noise lingering while trying to concentrate on a project, at the same time as holding a conversation with someone.

Maybe they also have a radio on in another room and some windows open, letting in even more external 'noise' to their workspace.

This, to me is a nightmare situation where productivity is concerned, as it is too much brain stimulation for me to fully function.

Yes - I am *that* person who will request that you turn down your own TV/stereo in your own home if you want me to have a decent conversation with you!

It just throws me off my train of thought!

- Listen to sounds that you do **enjoy** hearing.

Your favourite music, your favourite podcasts, films, voices, bird songs, waterfalls, waves crashing on the beach or sounds of laughter.

Do, see and hear more of what makes your heart sing.

SMELL more of the things you love.

- If the smell of a roast dinner gives you a warm, comforting feeling, then have more roast dinners!

- If your favourite air freshener or perfume lifts you up, spritz it to your heart's content.

- If the smell of the countryside makes you feel alive, spend more time outdoors, embracing the farm life!

TASTE more of what you love!

- If a treat from your favourite bakery makes you smile, grab one.

- If the fresh morning coffee makes you feel alert and ready to take on the day, then go ahead - enjoy it and smile as you taste and embrace the satisfaction you get from doing so!

Be mindful of how you **FEEL** when you are around different types of things, people and situations.

- If something or someone does not make you FEEL good, change the situation!

- Turn the TV off if you start to feel undesirable emotions, or if it brings back sad memories.

- Politely walk away from the person or conversation if they/it does not make you feel good.

- Put down the reading material if it is not serving you.

- Decline the social events that you do not want to attend.

- Wear what you want to wear.

- Think twice about agreeing to part with money for something that you are just not sure of.

If you do all of this with decorum, a smile and grace, then you are moving in the right direction for YOU and your own happiness.

Now I am well aware that unfortunate events happen to us all.

Sad news and sad events occur all around the world unfortunately, and I am not trying to mask all of this.

Our world can be cruel.

When we are going through our own tough times, it is important to monitor our own mindset and how we decide to deal with what is thrown our way.

Some personalities are 'strong-minded' and can push through the testing times with no issues at all.

Other personalities can hold onto negative feelings and struggle to see the light.

Seeing the bad in situations instead of the silver lining can even be a result of too much exposure to the wrong type of people and the wrong kind of events.

Fear of bad health, fear of death, fear of germs, fear of losing their job, fear of a relationship breakdown, fear of an accident happening...

These can all be by-products of repeated exposure to too many negative words, sad songs, sad programs, sad books, magazines, people, or conversations that they had in the past (which are still stuck in their head as a constant reminder).

Advertising, stories, billboards, leaflets and signs are all pushed in our faces daily.

You need to therefore be conscious of what topics and information your own mind tends to absorb and retain.

Do not let exposure of negative resources control your mind and/or your decisions.

Please also remember this when viewing 'perfect' social media posts, as social media content is often NOT a true reflection of that person's life.

People tend to share their best poses, best angles and best material items, but behind the public posts, things may not always be hunky dory.

This is why each and every individual on this planet MUST love themselves AS THEY ARE.

Not the edited version, not the airbrushed version and not the version in front of the mask.

God made us all in our own unique way and we need to thank God (or the Universe/Being or whatever you have chosen as your own preference) and show gratitude for our amazing bodies and our amazing lives.

Be sure to show gratitude for what you have **RIGHT NOW,** while working towards your next big goals and dreams.

We are all far from perfect, but we need to love our imperfect selves unconditionally.

As we evolve and better ourselves through life's lessons, the love and happiness will continually increase.

Make sure you love yourself more than anything else in the world, as without love for yourself, NO ONE else will see your best version of you.

Fact.

To reiterate - what you choose to watch, read, listen to or surround yourself with, has a profound effect on your mind, your mood and your success (or lack of).

I **choose** to watch happy, funny 'feel-good' films.

I do also watch the odd 'serious' stuff too, but I love to laugh and I therefore thoroughly enjoy a good, daft Adam Sandler comedy with the family at home.

Yes, you guessed it – I like to live in my own little happy bubble as much as I possibly can.

I take no shame in choosing to expose myself to all things good, all things positive, all things happy and all things shiny, pink and fluffy!

Most importantly, I am very happy and proud to now have an easily adaptable mindset that keeps negativity AWAY from me.

For this, I THANK YOU Universe and I thank ME!

- Believe in your superpowers.

- Love every inch of yourself (and everything around you) with the deepest passion you can find.

- Then watch amazing things happen.

We all have a choice in life and if you find that your feelings are negatively impacted after doing a certain thing, then do not do that thing anymore.

You are consciously CHOOSING bad feelings and a bad day by knowingly inviting things into your life that make you sad, angry or fearful.

Things you see, hear and experience implant visual memories in your brain, so why fill it with unwanted memories?

Remember - once you see something, it cannot be unseen.

Make the conscious effort to live a happy, amazing life and cut out anything that does not serve you.

Be more excited and inquisitive with every new experience that you have.

Ask, explore and enjoy.

It's time to start believing in magic!

CHAPTER 13

Mental Health

Today, more and more people are aware of the term 'mental health'.

On a positive note, this heightened awareness and the range of help and guidance that is now available, is great.

It means that support is available for individuals who need to effectively deal with the state of their own mental health.

What is not great however, is how many people still suffer in silence, scared to reach out to others for help.

There should be no stigma attached to pursuing self-help.

When we feel fragile, emotional, worried or fearful for our own health and our own wellbeing, we MUST take action and seek the relevant help.

Likewise, if you see someone else who needs support, lend them an ear and give them a smile.

Some warm, friendly human contact could be just what that person needs at that very moment in time.

All too often, we miss the signs that someone is struggling, because we may feel that it's 'not our place' to step in.

Just breaking down this barrier and asking if someone is ok could make the world of difference to their life.

Again, we can help ourselves (and others) by keeping an eye on our mindset, triggers, body language and happy places.

It is also important to not get stressed about things that you cannot control.

Some people get narked by the most insignificant things, like traffic, the weather, another person's attitude, not knowing where their phone is…

The list goes on.

I know people who refuse to walk over three consecutive grids on a pavement, as they fear it will bring them bad luck!

Where on earth is the logic in this?

Lots of people believe that seeing 1 magpie is bad luck.

Some people believe that breaking a mirror is bad luck, and they panic if this happens to them.

Please remember that a curse (or bad luck) is only as real as you allow it to be.

If the rainy weather is peeing you off, have a word with yourself and sort it out my friend!

Moaning or getting angry at the rain will not make the sun shine.

Whatever happens in life, accept it, laugh about it, and get on with your day.

I have had lots of fun walking my dog in the rain… and guess who else loves playing in the rain?

Children!

Remember how much fun it was playing in muddy puddles in those good old wellies and a funky raincoat!?

How amazing.

Why don't you go out and enjoy the rain like the young YOU would have?

If you feel the urge to experience that feeling all over again, just DO IT. It will be fun!

Embrace life in all seasons, no matter what the weather!

Getting dirty and muddy is great fun for all ages, so don't worry about mess, just stick it all in the washer and have a nice relaxing bath afterwards.

If you go ahead and make this happen on your next rainy day, you can enjoy that bath or shower even more, knowing that you have been spontaneous, daft and HAPPY that day.

That is what life is all about! Living in the moment and trying new things – all while not taking yourself too seriously.

Next time you feel yourself getting annoyed while sitting in traffic, just laugh at yourself for letting something so silly annoy you so much.

You can't magically shoo the cars away, so just breathe, get comfy, listen to some happy music and use the time to focus on your goals.

I used to be that person with road rage, and I would stress if I was sat in traffic while running late for something.

I now beam with smiles and say "thank you, thank you, thank you for my amazing life".

A little self-massage while you are at a standstill can also be great for lifting your mood.

Using the tapping method on your heart or applying circular motions to your temples can help relieve tension.

Remember to always put things into perspective.

If you are going through some challenging times, just know that these times will pass.

If you find yourself feeling anxious, stressed, depressed or just 'out of sorts', it may just be your body telling you to take a moment to slow down and reflect.

If you cannot find the strength to face anything on your day off, that is ok!

Get into bed and have a good sleep... and when you wake, you will feel much better.

We are all allowed those days where we don't get dressed.

I have duvet days where nothing gets done, then after an early night I wake feeling revived again.

Sometimes it may even take a number of days before you feel ready to take on the world again - and that is also fine!

Patience is a virtue and life shouldn't be a mad rush all the time.

Every day is a new day and with each new day comes new possibilities.

Recharge, rethink and re-plan for your greatness!

No matter what mask we choose to wear as a cover-up to our struggles, we all encounter sadness, rejection, loss and doubt.

Think twice before being so quick to judge someone else and if you find yourself judging yourself, please remind yourself of what you have been through and what you have achieved to get here.

Cruelty or gossip is NEVER a good idea, no matter how harmless you think it is.

This kind of behaviour changes the frequency of the environment, which of course, gets in the way of the good vibrations that we need to maintain for everyone's happiness.

If you know that deep down, you don't really have any major issues in your life currently, count your blessings, be resilient and avoid declaring illness, just because of the typical obstacles in life that everyone has to go through.

Remember - everyone goes through shit and upset, but seeing things from a different angle and coming out stronger is the aim.

Embrace the kind, helpful, thoughtful YOU and watch the world change for the better.

CHAPTER 14

Reignite the Magic!

Have you ever stopped and wondered when or why we lose our sense of fun and playfulness as we age?

I did, and that's when I decided to relive all the magic that I knew and loved throughout childhood.

I have even more of an excuse to see the world through a child's eyes again, as I have my darling Henry (and I make sure my son and I have the best adventures EVER together).

Making memories is so much more valuable than buying expensive material things that restrain the imaginations of so many children of the world today.

- What made your adrenalin pump when you were younger?
- What got you excited?
- Why did you stop doing the things you loved?

Unless there is a major health/physical factor affecting your abilities these days, there is NO reason why you can't reignite your passion for what you *used* to love.

Make sure you don't leave your best experiences in the past... Bring them to the present and the future!

I did, and I am now living my best life.

Homework

Make a list of all the things that you enjoyed as a child. Anything at all that made you smile and got you excited.

Again, I will share my own to give you a little nudge of inspiration:

- Ballet

I used to dance when I was a child. I danced in the local shows, displaying my best (she says!) jazz, tap, ballet and disco dancing skills – all while donning the most extravagant show attire!

For a while, I kept thinking about ballet. I kept looking online, I kept watching ballet and I kept envisioning myself doing ballet again.

I therefore decided to research local adult classes.... and then I took up a ballet course!

I had a new, elegant hobby to look forward to.

The short course helped to condition my body. It helped me to gain strength (both physically and mentally) and I also had a renewed respect for my body.

The respect I regained, included correcting my posture, making time for 'me', practising proper breathing techniques and de-stressing after busy workdays.

I also re-learned how powerful, flexible and adaptable our incredible bodies can be.

The feeling of grace and the beautiful classical music involved in it all, left me feeling revived and fulfilled after each class.

- The Theatre

I adore the theatre and love the elegance and music that surround all of the performances I see.

I therefore regularly go to the theatre with my mum and I have done for many years.

We watch everything from traditional operas and ballets, to pantos, comedies, tribute acts and many other sensational shows.

I love the atmosphere and the overwhelming feeling of satisfaction I get from being in the audience.

What kind of atmospheres do you like?

- Nature

The trees swaying in the wind, the birds cheerfully singing, and the glistening water in the rivers, lakes, canals and reservoirs are mesmerising to me.

Being in nature is one of life's best natural anti-depressants, stress-relivers and relaxers.

- Horse Riding

A previously mentioned hobby, but it's definitely a favourite of mine. I started horse riding when I was 4 and even though I broke my wrist falling when I was 11, the passion never died.

The fond memories and the excitement I get from all things horsey, is the reason I got back into it as an adult. I have had a few more falls since too!

- Reading Positive Books

I enjoyed reading as a child and was quite the bookworm. My preferred genres have certainly changed over the years, but if/when I read these days, you can almost guarantee it will be a positive, happy choice of book.

Being engrossed in a good book allows me to stay inspired.

- Feel-Good Films

Films like 'The Goonies' and 'The Karate Kid' are fab!

As a child, I loved movie nights and watching comical programmes together as a family. At the weekends, mum and dad would treat us to goodies from the 'Pop Man'. This was a guy who used to drive his mobile goody-shop down our cul-de-sac with exciting sugary treats and fizzy drinks! (An occasional treat for the tastebuds never hurt anyone!)

Programmes like 'Police Academy', 'The A Team' and 'The Only Fools and Horses' were amongst our childhood family faves!

I literally still ADORE watching all of these (over and over.... and over!) nowadays too, as I am filled with fond memories and lots of laughter when I do!

Laughter is ALWAYS a **MUST** for us all!

- Crystals

As a child, I loved sparkle. I loved pretty things and I loved dress jewellery.

These days, I am still an absolute sucker for pretty jewellery (although my choice pieces are now a lot more expensive!)

My sparkly chakra crystal collection is immense, but they all make me very happy, so long-live the crystal obsession!

Now it's your turn.

Make your own list as extensive as possible.

Dig deep to find those fun memories and keep adding to your list each time a new one pops up.

You can then refer to your list as the '***Catalogue of Fun Times***' and take your pick of things to do on a rainy day (or whenever you just want to go off, have some fun and be a big, excited kid again!)

There are no limits to what you and your body are capable of.

The only limits to how far you go, and how successful you become are your **OWN** doubts and/or lack of faith.

Your worst critique is yourself, so be sure to visualise your best self as if it were you NOW.

This way, you can truly **see** it, **believe** it and **make it your own true reality**.

- List your catalogue of fun times below.
- What made your adrenalin pump when you were younger?
- What got you excited?
- Can you relive these fun times again? If so, make sure you do.

_____

_____

Your Amazing Future

As we come to the end of 'The Magical World of YOU' I want to request that you keep the positivity flame alight.

Please do not let anyone dull your shine and do not give up at the first hurdle, the 5th set-back or the 10th failure.

Hopefully you don't get too many bumps in the road, but just remember that if you do, IT IS OK!

All millionaires, all entrepreneurs, all those people that you might currently see as 'having it easy' or having the 'best lives' will have experienced tough times!

Some of the most influential people out there have been through the worst possible scenarios in their own past lives... but they decided to create their own future by making happiness their priority (and never looking back).

You must remember to love yourself, live in the moment and use only positive affirmations.

Use only kind words when describing yourself, your beliefs, your talents and your individuality.

Homework

Think about the magical world of YOU.

Really think about how you have helped others this week, this month or this year.

Those little things you have done for others really do mean a lot.

- Did you offer an ear or a shoulder to someone who needed a friend?
- Did you provide a drink of water to someone who felt faint?

- Did you help to halt the bus that someone was running for?

- Did you reassure yourself (or someone else) that "everything is going to be alright"?

- Did you lend a stranger some change because they fell short at the till?

- Did you swap a shift at work with someone so that they did not miss a precious family occasion?

These small acts of kindness could be truly major things in someone else's eyes.

Remember that everyone is fighting a battle we know nothing about - and your helping hand at that precise moment could mark the turning point in their own future.

We can all be our own (and someone else's) hero... Every single day.

So – write them down.

I want you to write 10 answers to each of the following three questions:

- What positive things have you done for someone else this week?

List what it is that you did and how it has positively impacted the lives of others.

1
_____
_____
_____
_____
_____
2
_____
_____
_____
_____
_____

3

_____

_____

_____

4

_____

_____

_____

5

_____

_____

_____

6

_____

_____

_____

7

_____

_____

_____

8

_____

_____

_____

_____

9

_____

_____

_____

_____

10

_____

_____

_____

_____

Outro

Remember - there is no point having an amazing imagination without doing anything with it, so keep the vision going and keep the flames alight.

Conforming all the time to the norm could be tragic for your creative and colourful future, as it pushes down your own opinions and individuality.

We run the risk of becoming a world full of robots if we do not embrace life's true gifts.

- Instead of simple 'yes' or 'no' answers to questions, elaborate during conversations with people. Enjoy the exchanges of knowledge.

This will activate the brain more and allow you to explore and investigate intriguing new answers.

- Play with 'trial and error'.

Transferable skills that you learn along the way can always be applied to other projects if one doesn't quite work out.

Avoid competing with other people. Compete only with your past-self and with who you know you can become.

What are the key take aways from this book (for YOU personally)?

List them all below as your very own tailored wake up calls.

Once you have written your key words, quotes, reminders and action plans, you can work them into your daily routines.

This will ensure that your new positive traits become second nature.

1
_____

_____

_____

_____

2
_____

_____

_____

_____

3
_____

_____

_____

4 _____

_____

_____

_____

5 _____

_____

_____

_____

6 _____

_____

_____

_____

7 _____

_____

_____

_____

8 _____

_____

_____

_____

_____

9

_____

_____

_____

_____

10

_____

_____

_____

_____

Last Piece of Homework:

Get yourself an 'Idea Jar' when you feel your creativity has become stagnant or your invention is at a standstill.

Just write random words on lots of little pieces of folded paper and fill the jar with them. The first words that pop into your head!

When you need a moment of inspiration, pick a random word out of the jar, read the word out and run with it!

Think about that word deeply.

See what ideas or answers you get from really embracing the word itself and thinking about the possibilities associated with that word.

The universe is constantly giving us signs, so even if you happen to pull out the word 'chair', it could actually have real significant meaning for you and your work!

Good luck in your own perfect endeavours and enjoy the ride while embarking on your new and improved, individual journey.

Wishing you a wonderful life, filled with laughter, kindness, health and wealth.

I hope you have enjoyed reading my book and if so, your positive thoughts, wishes and support would be greatly appreciated.

I would love to see your book selfies and hear all about your own achievements!

The universe may bring us together in the future, but if you would like to connect sooner, feel free to drop me a note:

Email:

sarahmarieholl277@gmail.com

themagicalworldofyou@gmail.com

Instagram:

@ladysarahmarie

@themagicalworldofyou

Thank you.

The Magical World of YOU! is a straight-talking wake-up call for anyone who needs a push to achieve their dreams.

From practical advice, to personal anecdotes and simple homework, this is the self-help manual you didn't know you needed!

So stop procrastinating and turn those wishes into reality.

Rediscover yourself, know your worth and achieve your goal of living a happier, healthier life.

Printed in Great Britain
by Amazon

37454976R00057